U.S. Department of Justice
Office of Justice Programs
Office for Victims of Crime

D1466920

USING GEOGRAPHIC INFORMATION SYSTEMS TO MAP CRIME VICTIM SERVICES

A Guide for State Victims of Crime Act
Administrators and Victim Service Providers

Office for Victims of Crime
OVC
"Putting Victims First"

NIJ
NATIONAL
INSTITUTE
of JUSTICE

U.S. Department of Justice
Office of Justice Programs
810 Seventh Street N.W.
Washington, DC 20531

John Ashcroft
Attorney General

Deborah J. Daniels
Assistant Attorney General

John W. Gillis
Director, Office for Victims of Crime

Office of Justice Programs
World Wide Web Home Page
www.ojp.usdoj.gov

Office for Victims of Crime
World Wide Web Home Page
www.ojp.usdoj.gov/ovc

For grant and funding information, contact
U.S. Department of Justice Response Center
1–800–421–6770

OVC Resource Center
1–800–627–6872
(TTY 1–877–712–9279)
www.ncjrs.org

OVC Training and Technical Assistance Center
1–866–682–8822
(TTY 1–866–682–8880)
www.ojp.usdoj.gov/ovc/assist/welcome html

NCJ 191877

Preparation of this document was supported by the Office for Victims of Crime,
Office of Justice Programs, U.S. Department of Justice. The Office for Victims of
Crime is a component of the Office of Justice Programs, which also includes the
Bureau of Justice Assistance, the Bureau of Justice Statistics, the National Institute
of Justice, and the Office of Juvenile Justice and Delinquency Prevention.

USING GEOGRAPHIC INFORMATION SYSTEMS TO MAP CRIME VICTIM SERVICES

A Guide for State Victims of Crime Act Administrators and Victim Service Providers

by

Debra A. Stoe, Acting Director

Mapping and Analysis for Public Safety

(formerly the Crime Mapping Research Center)

National Institute of Justice

with

Carol R. Watkins, Special Assistant to the OVC Director

Jeffrey Kerr, Program Specialist

Linda Rost, Administrative Specialist

State Compensation and Assistance Division

Office for Victims of Crime

and

Theodosia Craig, Writer/Editor

Aspen Systems Corporation

February 2003
NCJ 191877

Message From the Director of the Office for Victims of Crime

As more crime victims exercise their rights and seek services, state Victims of Crime Act (VOCA) crime victim compensation and assistance administrators and victim service providers are challenged to assess victim needs, allocate available resources effectively, and advocate for additional resources. Since the 1986 infusion of federal VOCA funds, many victim service programs have been established and preexisting ones have grown. During the past 15 years, state legislatures have raised funding for crime victim compensation and assistance, increasing the money available to victims and victim services. At the same time, field reports indicate that obtaining sufficient funds is a continuing challenge as we reach out to previously unserved victims.

Because of its growth, the victim service field is improving its administrative and management skills. Calls from policymaking bodies and the public for accountability on the use of public funds have led to an examination of tools that can support data-driven decisionmaking and outcome evaluation. To provide state administrators and victim service providers with one such tool for assessment, planning, and operations, the Office for Victims of Crime (OVC) has partnered with the National Institute of Justice (NIJ) Mapping and Analysis for Public Safety (MAPS), formerly the Crime Mapping Research Center, to introduce Geographic Information Systems (GIS) technology to the victim service field.

GIS technology can help analyze information, such as types of crime by location, victim population groups served and underserved, and the location of victim service organizations and their geographic service areas. This information can be used to examine the availability of basic services and the sufficiency of services for specialized population groups. It can visually display multiple funding sources in a geographic area to help in fair distribution of resources. It can be extremely useful in developing strategic program and financial plans for the maintenance and development of victim services.

OVC is honored to work with NIJ to publish this valuable report. We also wish to extend our appreciation to individuals in the states and municipalities that provided the data used to create maps for this report. Our hope is that you will find GIS and this report useful in your efforts to advance crime victim services.

John W. Gillis, Director
Office for Victims of Crime

MESSAGE FROM THE DIRECTOR OF THE NATIONAL INSTITUTE OF JUSTICE

For more than a decade, the criminal justice community has realized the valuable analytic benefits of Geographic Information Systems (GIS). This powerful technology enhances the ability of researchers and practitioners to identify problem areas and target scarce resources. To promote the use of GIS throughout the criminal justice system, the National Institute of Justice (NIJ) established Mapping and Analysis for Public Safety (MAPS), formerly the Crime Mapping Research Center, in 1997. A year later, NIJ created the Crime Mapping and Analysis Program, a training resource at the National Law Enforcement and Corrections Technology Center–Rocky Mountain, in Denver, Colorado. NIJ's investment in crime mapping was timely because the value of GIS had been demonstrated with early successes in the analysis of criminal behavior. As a result, NIJ has supported the allocation of resources, the organization of data, and the evaluation of programs and initiatives to increase awareness of GIS as a crime-fighting tool.

NIJ's crime-mapping efforts have yielded five national conferences on the study and use of crime mapping, each drawing more than 600 attendees. MAPS conducts research in the field of analytic crime mapping and offers guidance and leadership to criminal justice agencies nationwide. In addition, MAPS promotes, evaluates, develops, and disseminates GIS technology. Through partnerships and other federally funded programs, NIJ has helped develop crime-mapping software. Some software applications can be downloaded free from the MAPS Web site at www.ojp.usdoj.gov/nij/maps.

Although great strides have been made in disseminating GIS technology to local law enforcement agencies, NIJ continues to explore new uses for GIS in the criminal justice field.

One natural application NIJ is focusing on is the more efficient allocation of victims' services and resources.

This report introduces GIS to state Victims of Crime Act (VOCA) administrators and victim service providers to improve the methods by which victim compensation and victim assistance are provided to states. VOCA administrators will learn how to manage the strategic planning efforts behind crime mapping and how GIS can serve as a key vehicle in the decisionmaking process.

Sarah V. Hart, Director
National Institute of Justice

CONTENTS

CRIME MAPPING

he use of Geographic Information Systems (GIS) in the criminal justice field has its roots in the earlier generation of police crime maps. Historically, law enforcement agencies and other organizations used hardcopy pin maps to chart criminal activity; but these maps were static and, as crime rates increased, difficult to maintain. In recent years, with advances in quick and user-friendly software, manual pin mapping has given way to computerized crime mapping.

GIS is an application that links database[1] software to graphics software to create visual images of various types of data in map format. It is a unique tool for analyzing physical space and conveying perspective. Presenting data in the form of a map helps agencies understand the significance of where, when, and by whom crimes are committed.

Technological advancements have enabled agencies to collect enormous amounts of data. In the law enforcement field, a rise in crime and an increase in the number of calls for service have led to a greater need to sort, organize, analyze, and disseminate data. As a result, criminal justice agencies are turning to GIS software and the latest crime-mapping techniques to deliver data in a more efficient and instructive manner. In addition, using GIS to map crime and criminal behavior eliminates the rampant duplication of efforts among agencies.

This has prompted the introduction and application of GIS technologies in the victim service field. Consequently, there is a growing need to educate and guide agencies that rely on other means of recording their data in the direction of implementing GIS. For example, if a VOCA compensation administrator wants to create a visual depiction of the location of applicants, street addresses and other relevant information can be converted into a database format and linked to a graphics software application. In this example, the link is based on the street address. Other spatial or geographic identifiers[2] that could be used include ZIP Codes and census tracts.[3] This particular example would allow administrators to analyze locations that generate victim compensation claims. Areas that lack applications could be examined to determine whether additional applications can be generated and if administrators need to plan for outreach to those areas.

GIS software represents data on a map using points, lines, and polygons.[4] Features that can be represented as points include streetlight poles, crime events, and bus stops. Bus routes, streets, and rivers are usually represented using lines; counties, states, and ZIP Codes are depicted using polygons. GIS software is designed to capture, store, manage, integrate, and manipulate various layers of data, allowing the user to visualize and analyze the data in a spatial environment (exhibit 1).

Exhibit 1: Graphics Representing Data

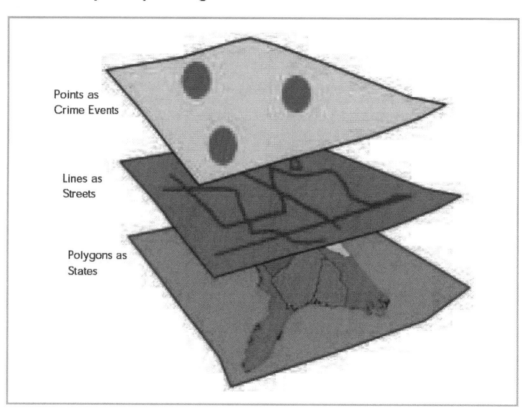

Points as
Crime Events

Lines as
Streets

Polygons as
States

Most GIS applications contain base information that orients the map to the reader. Some examples of base information include roads and state and county boundaries. One easy way to visualize base layers is to think about the information found in a road atlas.

In GIS, a database can represent a layer of information and that can be expanded to create additional layers. For example, the OVC Subgrant Award Report System (SARS) could be one layer, with the location of all subgrantees defined as individual points on that layer. Another layer of data could be added by querying the SARS database for a particular type of service provider, such as programs for survivors of homicide victims. This additional layer would be mapped using a different color or graphic symbol.

The real power of GIS is that it gives users the ability to analyze multiple layers of information. Not only can users create additional layers from a single database, they can also integrate disparate datasets[5] from other sources such as police departments, planning and
housing agencies, and the tax assessor's office (exhibit 2). Each agency's data would
become another layer of information in GIS. With this layering of information, users can discern spatial relationships among previously disassociated data. For example, the layer of
SARS information could be overlaid with incidents of domestic violence data from local
police departments about locations of courts handling domestic violence cases and locations
of public transportation systems. With this displayed information, users could examine how
accessible services and the criminal justice system are for domestic violence victims.

Exhibit 2: Multiple Layers of Information

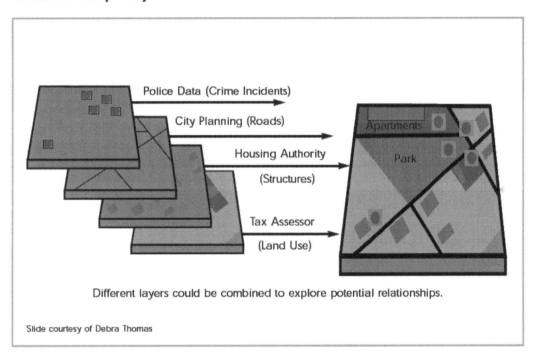

Police Data (Crime Incidents)

City Planning (Roads)

Housing Authority

(Structures)

Tax Assessor

(Land Use)

Apartments

Park

Different layers could be combined to explore potential relationships.

Slide courtesy of Debra Thomas

GIS can pinpoint the physical location of features[6] in every layer. It allows an administrator
to conduct spatial searches or queries in addition to tabular database queries. For example,
a tabular database query can retrieve information about the increase or decrease in the
number of crime victim compensation claims submitted in a particular region. What a tabular query cannot show is whether there has been a spatial displacement or diffusion of
claims. In other words, has the number of claims remained the same but shifted from one
neighborhood to another, or has the number of claims been diffused due to additional
resources in an area?

Another example of a spatial search would be to determine the proximity of one location to
another. For instance, one dataset or layer shows school locations, while another indicates

crime locations involving juveniles. Overlaying this data in GIS, users can identify crimes that occurred within 1,000 feet of a school. This information can be used to determine where services could be located most effectively (exhibit 3) and could lead to an understanding of the spatial relationship between crimes and school locations.

Although GIS software packages can be purchased containing base information such as streets and census data, most GIS also require agency-specific data. A VOCA administrator could tailor a GIS to fit his or her requirements by populating it with other data, such as VOCA subgrantee service areas, which could be used to examine statewide coverage or

Exhibit 3: Spatial Search

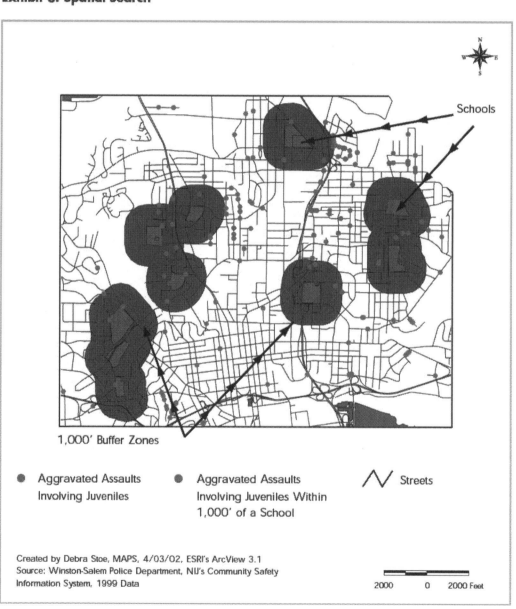

Schools

1,000' Buffer Zones

● Aggravated Assaults Involving Juveniles

● Aggravated Assaults Involving Juveniles Within 1,000' of a School

/\/ Streets

Created by Debra Stoe, MAPS, 4/03/02, ESRI's ArcView 3.1
Source: Winston-Salem Police Department, NIJ's Community Safety
Information System, 1999 Data

2000   0   2000 Feet

types of crime to plan for general or specialized services. In summary, GIS is a powerful mapping tool that allows agencies to identify their data spatially to better analyze data relationships.

If an agency collects data via Excel, Access, Quattro Pro, Paradox, Oracle, SQL Server, or any other type of spreadsheet or database management system, the data have potential for use in GIS, but must have a geographic reference. Generally, ZIP Codes, street addresses, or x–y coordinates are used to link data to the map by geocoding, or plotting on a map, the data. For example (exhibit 4), a street address such as 1150 Main Street can be matched against a street centerline[7] file to determine its location. The geocoding function will link an address to its approximate location on the street segment based on its number. For example, 1150 Main Street would be placed on the even side of the street about halfway between the 1100 and 1200 blocks.

Exhibit 4: Geocoding Addresses

To protect private and confidential information, sensitive data are geocoded to the street block, ZIP Code, or census-tract level rather than the street level to reduce the possibility of identifying an individual from the mapped data.

Creating Maps

Crime mapping has its roots in cartography[8] and comes with its own set of rules and limitations. When publishing an article, authors always cite information resources. When constructing a map, cartographers always cite the source of the data and the software used to create the map. If citations are left out, the map is incomplete and users may misinterpret the information displayed. It is also recommended that mapmakers include disclaimers and/or additional information to eliminate any misinterpretation of the material. A variety of maps can be created using GIS software, but the three most common are pin maps, thematic maps, and association or integrated maps.

Pin Maps

Pin maps—which use push pins to identify important locations—have long helped police officers patrol neighborhoods and detectives investigate crimes. GIS enables law enforcement agencies to create, update, duplicate, and distribute pin maps more efficiently and easily. Administrators of VOCA victim assistance can plot the locations of victim service providers on pin maps to identify gaps in and duplication of services. Victim service providers can display the vicinity of crime victims to better coordinate their efforts with other providers. The pin map is one of the easiest maps to create. Exhibit 5 shows the locations of all homicides that occurred in Washington, D.C., in 1994 and 1995. During the 2-year period, there were 756 murders and all but one occurred east of the Rock Creek Park.[9] Although the points on the map only show location, they reveal a spatial significance that cannot be discerned using a tabular query.

Exhibit 5: Homicides in Washington, DC 1994–95

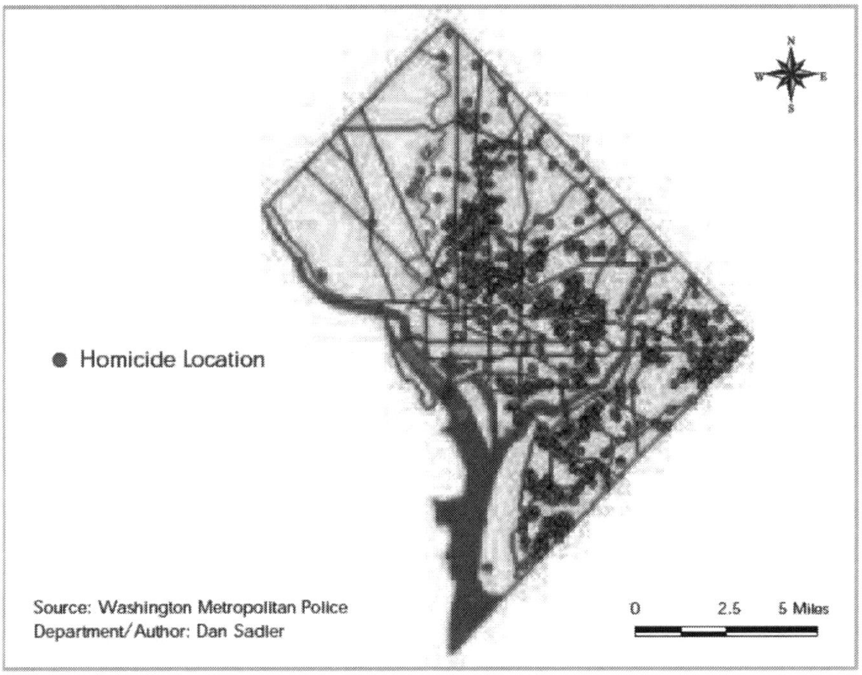

● Homicide Location

Source: Washington Metropolitan Police
Department/Author: Dan Sadler

0   2.5   5 Miles

Thematic Maps

A thematic map can identify the density value of a particular attribute, such as the number of assaults, crime victim service centers, or victim compensation claims in a geographically defined boundary composed of a state, police precinct, county, neighborhood, census tract, or victim service provider catchment area (see exhibit 10). In exhibit 6, density values are used to create a map, with shaded colors representing the different values between the boundaries, that allows users to examine patterns across selected boundaries. The shading of thematic maps ranges from light to dark, with the lightest shade representing the lowest value and the darkest shade representing the highest value. Exhibit 6 shows the density of California VOCA subgrantees by county.

Association or Integrated Maps

Association or integrated maps are usually a combination of a pin map and a thematic map. Exhibit 7 combines data from North Carolina's Winston-Salem Police Department (WSPD), the Winston-Salem Housing Department, and the U.S. Census Bureau. In this map, aggravated assaults and public housing units are identified with points, while the population demographics are represented with various shades of the same color and organized by police district boundaries.

This map spatially contextualizes[10] the data. Here, WSPD chose to view census data reaggregated to police beat boundaries. With this type of map, WSPD can view income, population, gender, race, and other factors within the boundaries that represent the department's work environment. Winston-Salem manages and allocates police department resources by police districts. By reaggregating census data, information has been made more applicable to department needs. For instance, WSPD may choose to increase resources in communities with large numbers of public housing units. Integrated crime mapping allows WSPD to make strategic administrative decisions based on contextualized data.

How GIS Is Used in Law Enforcement

GIS does not replace a law enforcement agency's process of collecting and storing information in a database. Rather, it enhances the agency's ability to use the data. However, the use

Exhibit 6: Density of California VOCA Subgrantees

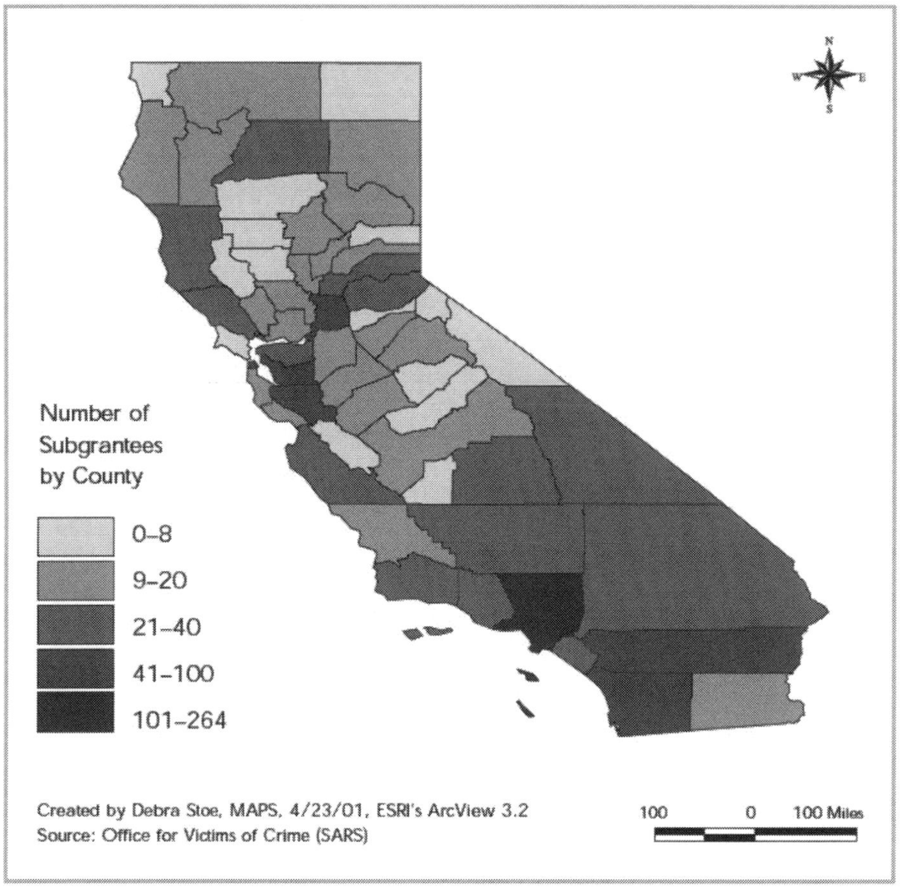

Number of Subgrantees by County

- 0–8
- 9–20
- 21–40
- 41–100
- 101–264

Created by Debra Stoe, MAPS, 4/23/01, ESRI's ArcView 3.2
Source: Office for Victims of Crime (SARS)

100   0   100 Miles

of contextualization raises new concerns about the need for privacy and confidentiality guidelines.

For example, a map can be created to show when and where a crime occurred with what type of weapon was used, whether a victim was present, whether the victim was male or female, and so forth. Once data, such as the income level of Hispanic females between ages 18 and 25, is entered into a GIS database, the user can overlay that information with a specific crime, such as recent homicides or rapes occurring in the neighborhood between 8 p.m. and midnight. Overlaying specific crimes with ethnicity, age, and gender may inadvertently reveal the

---

Questions To Consider (Exhibit 6)

❱ Is the density of subgrantees consistent with population?

❱ Is the density of subgrantees consistent with the crime rate?

❱ What types of services are provided in all counties?

❱ Where are the gaps?

Exhibit 7: Winston-Salem, NC

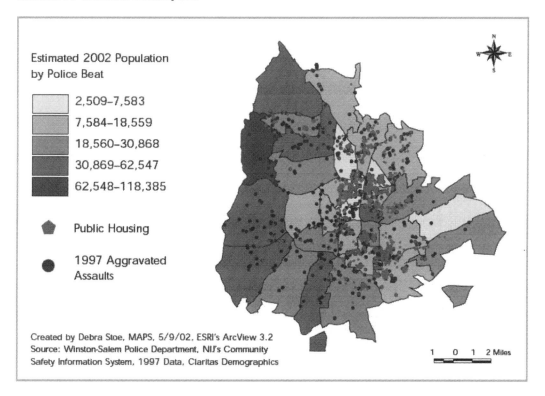

Estimated 2002 Population
by Police Beat

2,509–7,583
7,584–18,559
18,560–30,868
30,869–62,547
62,548–118,385

Public Housing

1997 Aggravated Assaults

Created by Debra Stoe, MAPS, 5/9/02, ESRI's ArcView 3.2
Source: Winston-Salem Police Department, NIJ's Community
Safety Information System, 1997 Data, Claritas Demographics

1 0 1 2 Miles

identity of a victim. Therefore, the creators of GIS data layers must be aware of confidential and sensitive data and the need to take precautions to protect victims' rights and privacy.

GIS usage enhances a police officer's time on the streets. An officer with access to GIS software and additional datasets, such as parolee and probationer data, can run queries from a laptop in the patrol car using the Community Policing Beat Book. The Community Policing Beat Book is a crime-mapping tool created by Environmental Systems Research Institute (ESRI), funded by NIJ,[11] and tailored for law enforcement agencies. Officers can use it to check how many parolees or probationers were recently released on their beat, the conditions of their release, and if they have violated any of these conditions.

In 1998, the U.S. Department of Justice launched the Strategic Approaches to Community Safety Initiative, a multiagency collaborative approach to reduce crime in communities by using data-driven problem solving. One major component of this project has been the development of the Community Safety Information System (CSIS), a GIS that provides spatial analysis capabilities for addressing crime. Exhibit 7 is an integrated map created from CSIS data collected in Winston-Salem, North Carolina, the pilot site for the initiative.

In addition to plotting the geographical attributes of criminal phenomena, law enforcement agencies seek answers to why a specific crime occurs in a certain area. In 1982, George L. Kelling and James Q. Wilson developed the Broken Windows theory to describe the relationship between disorder and crime in a neighborhood. They concluded that as the physical environment in a neighborhood deteriorates the crime rate increases. Newly opened adult bookstores selling pornographic materials, check cashing stores, and vacant housing are predictors of declining neighborhoods. By highlighting aspects of a crime on a map with

Questions To Consider (Exhibit 7)

▶ Are a sufficient number of claims being generated based on this assault data?

▶ Where are hospital emergency rooms located?

▶ Are admission staff trained in compensation?

▶ Is there a victim advocate in the police department in areas with higher assault rates?

▶ Are other state and federal resources, in addition to victim compensation and assistance, being integrated in the public housing communities?

Exhibit 8: Crime Mapping Registered Child Sex Offenders

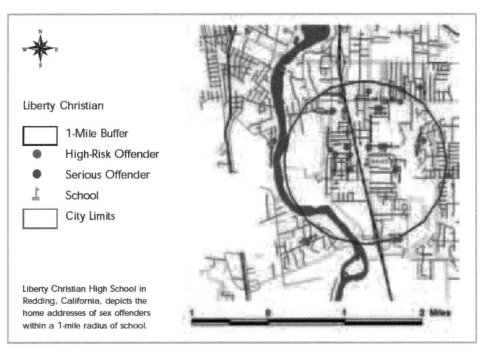

Liberty Christian

☐ 1-Mile Buffer

● High-Risk Offender

● Serious Offender

⚑ School

☐ City Limits

Liberty Christian High School in Redding, California, depicts the home addresses of sex offenders within a 1-mile radius of school.

Disclaimer: Please note that the symbols identifying the street location *do not* represent the exact location of where the offender lives. The symbols have been enlarged and offset to keep an exact location from being determined. This map can be found at http://ci.redding.ca.us/rpd/rpdmap_libertychristian.html.

neighborhood attributes, crime analysts can contextualize the data and gain insight about why crimes occur.

Some law enforcement agencies use crime mapping to show where registered child sex offenders live. They compare the locations of child sex offenders with the locations of the town's schools. A buffer zone is drawn around each school to observe how close the known offenders live to these potential target areas. The sheriff's department in San Bernardino County, California, is one agency that uses this technique. Exhibit 8 shows how the Redding Police Department in Redding, California, uses this technique to map registered child sex offenders.

One department goal is to register sex offenders with local law enforcement, a requirement under Section 290 of the California Penal Code. Another goal has been to arrest individuals who have violated the conditions of their parole or probation. In 1999, 3 of 36 targeted registrants were arrested for noncompliance with the penal code or some violation of parole or probation. In addition, county officers issued warrants for 25 other registrants. For more details, check out *Crime Mapping Case Studies: Successes in the Field*, Volume 2 (La Vigne and Wartell, 2000).

Similarly, a victim service provider could use GIS to track and map the location of both offenders and/or victims who were issued protection orders in stalking cases. GIS software can map the home address of an individual, taking into consideration the conditions of the protection order associated with the offender. Distance buffers can then be drawn around these locations and reveal violations or compliance with the specified restrictions.

How State VOCA Administrators Can Use GIS

State VOCA administrators can use GIS in many ways. As an analytical tool, GIS can identify trends and patterns not discernible by tabular inquiries. An example would be exploring the relationship between addresses of applicants for crime victim compensation and locations of crime to learn whether an appropriate number of applications is being submitted from neighborhoods with high crime rates.

GIS facilitates data-driven decisionmaking. By using multiple-source data, administrators can analyze problems in greater depth. For example, integrating information on subgrants funded by VOCA victim assistance, the Violence Against Women Act (VAWA), the Centers for Disease Control and Prevention's Rape Prevention and Education Grant Program, and the U.S. Department of Health and Human Services, Family Violence Prevention Funds into one data warehouse can be key to developing a statewide financial plan for victim services. GIS can be used in operations by using its funding data to determine which organizations will receive VOCA victim assistance grants.

Because GIS can track changes over time, it can evaluate strategies. If a VOCA victim assistance administrator responds to requests for increased services in African-American communities by developing plans for delivering services and awarding grants to appropriate organizations, the administrator can track the use of services from those grants on a regular basis. If certain programs are accessed as expected and others are not, the administrator can use this information to ask questions about the patterns of use and explore further options.

Administrators can use GIS to disseminate information to advisory groups and the public and to conduct legislative analysis. GIS can be used to coordinate services with other agencies and organizations, as in child abuse investigation and treatment teams that include cross-jurisdictional involvement of law enforcement, prosecution, child protective services, and health and mental health services.

In summary, GIS can be a valuable tool in helping administrators implement a comprehensive and seamless service delivery system for crime victims.

How Administrators of VOCA Victim Assistance Can Use GIS

Several factors can influence where and why crime occurs, including the distance from an offender's residence, familiarity with his or her surroundings, and accessibility to and knowledge of the victim (www.ojp.usdoj.gov/cmrc/briefing book/whymap.html). Therefore, mapping incidents of crime, locations of crime victims, and potential crime hot spots can help in making decisions about where to locate victim services.

As previously mentioned, one of the more recognized GIS capabilities is its visual display of information. For many individuals, information that is spatially displayed is more easily communicated and understood. GIS can improve presentation of information at planning, policy, and funding meetings by displaying the information in various formats, such as maps, reports, and tables accompanied by descriptive narratives.

To illustrate mapping crime victim services as an administrative tool, the State of California is depicted in exhibits 9 and 10. The data source used is the OVC SARS database. Subgrantees are geocoded by their ZIP Codes using ESRI's ArcView 3.2 software. Using a pin map, one can identify areas where available services are more densely located (exhibit 9). This overview of the state is a starting point that will provide information to further develop regional analysis.

Victim assistance administrators can plot the catchment areas of victim service providers on a map along with the victim population groups served. Overlaying this information with the types of crimes committed can help determine what additional services are needed in which locations for underserved groups.

For example, areas with many reports of crimes against the elderly may need specialized services. Using law enforcement crime reports and calls-for-service information, VOCA

Exhibit 9: Locations of Subgrantees in California

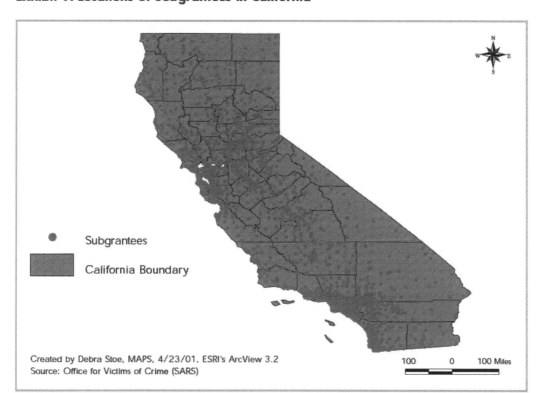

Created by Debra Stoe, MAPS, 4/23/01, ESRI's ArcView 3.2
Source: Office for Victims of Crime (SARS)

Disclaimer: This map represents 206 ZIP Codes and 82 percent of the California subgrantees.

Crime Mapping

Exhibit 10: 1999 California's Hispanic Population and OVC Subgrantees

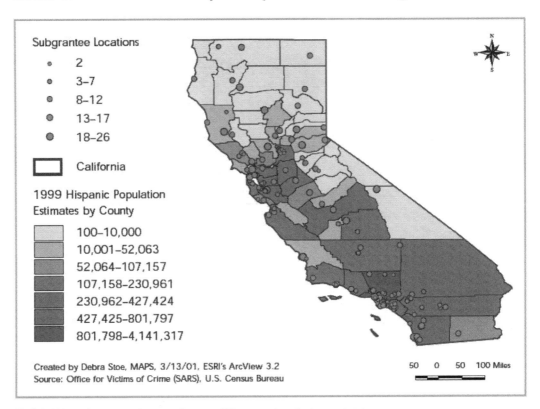

Disclaimer: This map represents 206 ZIP Codes and 82 percent of the California subgrantees.

administrators can examine areas where the greatest density of these incidents occur and overlay this information with the locations and use rates of existing victim services, senior housing, senior citizen centers, meals-on-wheels programs, and other services. VOCA assistance administrators can use this information to work with these organizations to establish needed services.

When administrators must manage or coordinate multiple funding sources that cross legal boundaries (e.g., states, Indian Country, neighborhoods, or cities), GIS can help them better allocate the funds by creating a map of current funding and developing other maps to demonstrate statewide coverage of victim services. This is done by using GIS to reconfigure the distribution of funds. Using the previous example of crimes against elders, victim services funding can be coordinated with other funding for elder services to create a more accessible and victim-friendly system.

In exhibit 10, GIS mapping reveals how accessible services are to minority crime victims. It shows estimates of California's Hispanic population and the locations of subgrantees. Administrators can use this information to determine which programs must have the bilingual and bicultural capacity to provide services to this ethnic group.

A GIS containing census data on Hispanics, African-Americans, Asians, and Native Americans can help administrators plan for delivery of services in these communities. This information can be linked to other maps with specific features, such as jurisdictional boundaries, public transportation routes, sites accessible to people with disabilities, and geographic terrain that complicates service delivery. Administrators can use this information to plan service development and outreach.

In the next map, we move from a state to a much smaller area, the City of New Haven, Connecticut (exhibit 11). This map shows the locations of VOCA-funded subgrantees and raises questions about what other services are available for crime victims. Additional research resulted in the new map (exhibit 12), which shows 21 additional service locations, reflecting much greater coverage.

To provide a comprehensive picture of available services, additional contextual mapping could add layers of provider agencies' service areas and of the public transportation system in relation to courts, police stations and substations, and residential areas.

The next example shows the location of VOCA subgrantees covering the states of California and Nevada in a variation on the pin map (exhibit 13). Graduated symbols are used to

Exhibit 11: Locations of 1997 and 1998 Subgrantees in New Haven, CT

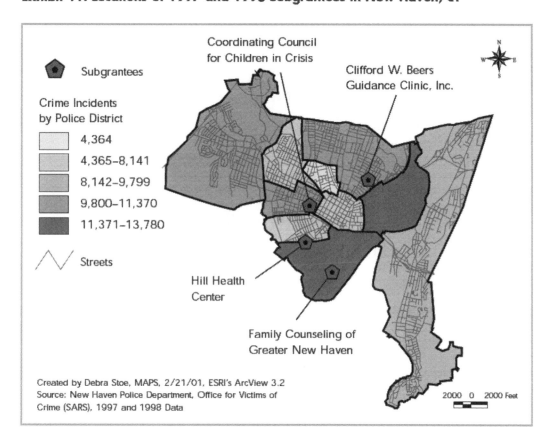

Exhibit 12: Locations of VOCA and Other Service Providers in New Haven, CT

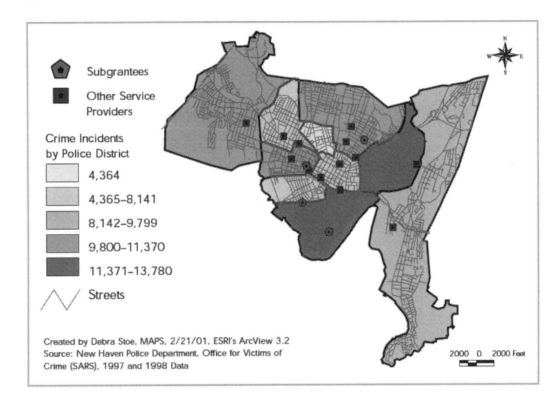

Exhibit 13: Identifying Coverages Across California/Nevada State Boundaries

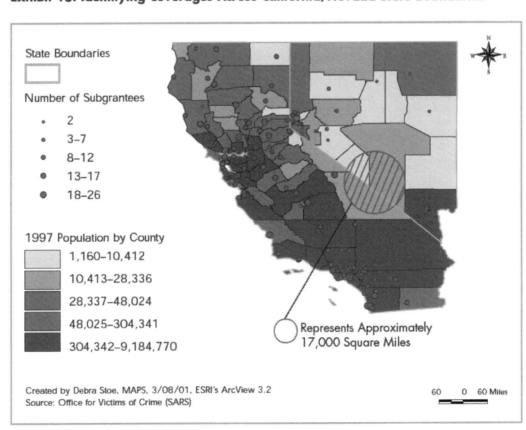

indicate ZIP Codes that contain more than one subgrantee. The larger the circle, the greater the number of points located within the polygon. In this case, the number of subgrantees within a ZIP Code varies from 1 to 26. Five different sizes of circles are used to indicate various groupings (0–2, 3–7, 8–12, 13–17, 18–26). This map uses 169 geocoded ZIP Codes.

Bordering states that do not share information are limited in their ability to ascertain whether adjacent geographical areas are adequately served. Communicating and sharing spatial data across state boundaries and between agencies minimizes the duplication of services, allowing administrators to maximize services to areas where the rate and types of victimization exceed the services available. Conversely, noted in this map is a 17,000-square-mile area with no visible subgrantee—a point of consideration for both California and Nevada administrators.

Exhibit 14 is another example of an effective use of maps. It shows three images of Nevada that show changes in population by areas of the state. Note the results of slow but steady growth between 1990 and 1999 in the northeast and southwest. This information can affect decisions on how best to allocate funds statewide.

With GIS, an administrator could quickly add several years of population data with service locations to discern whether the population density has increased or decreased in proximity to services provided, possibly explaining a change in victims served. An overlay indicating recent changes in transportation routes could explain why there had been an increase in those seeking assistance. GIS can quickly produce multiple scenarios by integrating and overlaying disparate datasets, allowing for a wide array of possibilities for analysis and support for strategic planning.

Exhibit 14: Nevada's Changes in Population

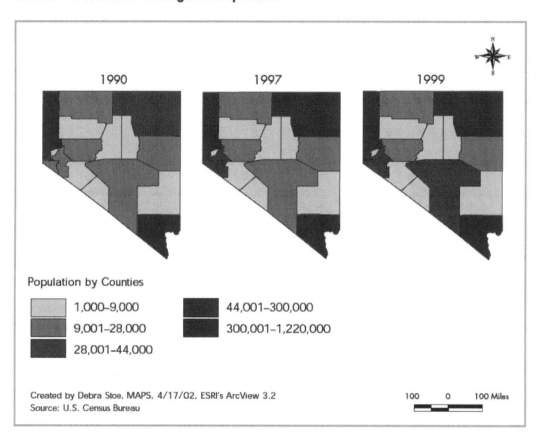

How Administrators
of VOCA Victim Compensation Can Use GIS

Administrators of VOCA crime victim compensation may be interested in several of the
preceding exhibit maps. The map showing California subgrantees can be overlaid with
data from crime victim compensation claims to examine whether subgrantees are generating expected claims. Using the map showing the changes in the population of Nevada,
administrators can examine whether there is an increase in crime and a commensurate
increase in claims in areas with increased populations. They can use this information to
plan outreach activities.

The true benefits of GIS technology are realized when data are shared and integrated into
an organization's daily operations. With access to crime data, administrators of VOCA
crime victim compensation can quickly identify the locations of crime and crime victims. They
can then more accurately predict the numbers and types of claims that will be generated
from those locations. Exhibit 15 indicates the number of crime victims who received compensation in relation to the location of crimes in Pittsburgh, Pennsylvania, and shows that applications are not coming from the areas where crime occurs. Discrepancies in the data may
occur, however, if victims use their resident addresses to apply for compensation rather than
the addresses of where the crime occurred. For more information, administrators of crime victim compensation could overlay a map of subgrantees with a map of claims applications to

**Exhibit 15: 1999 Crime Incidents in Pittsburgh, PA, and Recipients of
Victim Compensation**

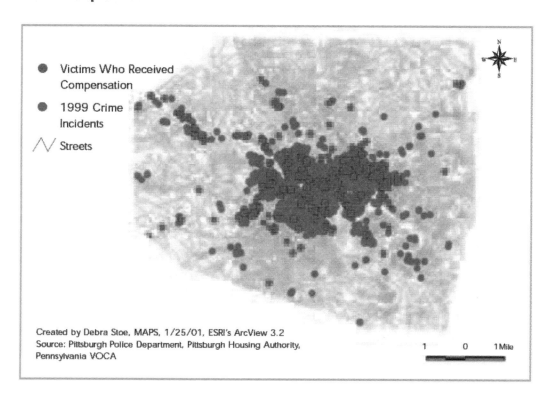

Victims Who Received
Compensation

1999 Crime
Incidents

Streets

Created by Debra Stoe, MAPS, 1/25/01, ESRI's ArcView 3.2
Source: Pittsburgh Police Department, Pittsburgh Housing Authority,
Pennsylvania VOCA

1   0   1 Mile

see if subgrantees are generating a sufficient number of applications.

Administrators of crime victim compensation can use the information on VAWA grants as shown in the State of Georgia (exhibit 16) to identify counties where additional service providers may be available to make referrals.

Questions To Consider (Exhibit 15)

▶ What is the frequency of crime incidents and the frequency of victims receiving compensation?

▶ How does this information affect outreach planning?

How Subgrantees, Crime Victim Assistance Coalitions, and Victim Service Providers Can Use Crime Mapping

Crime victim services subgrantees, coalitions, and providers can use GIS to study crime rates and resources in specific areas to improve allocation of resources, such as placing victim advocates in community centers, police departments, or courts. When gaps in services are

Exhibit 16: Georgia Areas Served by VAWA Domestic Violence and Sexual Assault Service Projects

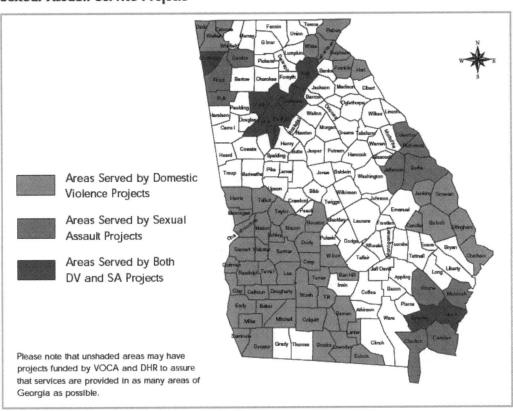

Areas Served by Domestic Violence Projects

Areas Served by Sexual Assault Projects

Areas Served by Both DV and SA Projects

Please note that unshaded areas may have projects funded by VOCA and DHR to assure that services are provided in as many areas of Georgia as possible.

identified, grant writers can incorporate this data into applications for federal, state, local, and foundation funding, thus documenting the scope of the problem for proposal reviewers.

GIS technology uses a process called buffering to create a barrier or zone around an area to be investigated or analyzed. For example, victims of domestic violence need many different services and are often dependent on public transportation in urban areas. In this instance, coalitions and service providers may want to buffer[12] the area surrounding bus routes to determine how accessible police departments, shelters, courts, and social services are to victims of domestic violence. Networking[13] is another process used to calculate optimum travel distances from all service locations or to determine optimum minimum distances between service locations.

Sexual assault coalitions can develop maps of assault locations, offering a broader look at where assaults occur or where victims reside. Child abuse coalitions can map the location of registered child molesters and overlay this information with data on the locations of schools and playgrounds to ensure supervision of offenders and protection of children (see exhibits 3 and 8).

State coalitions for crime victim assistance and providers of victim services can use GIS to identify underserved victims of crime, such as victims of physical assault, burglary, robbery, drunk driving, arson, and hate crime, and victims who are family members of homicide victims. This information can be shared among several groups working to plan for and serve these populations. This powerful tool allows the various coalitions to jointly assess and analyze crime on a larger scale by producing maps that can be shared and allow for joint strategic planning to develop a seamless delivery system for crime victims.

Mapping Victim Services

When creating a mapping system for crime victim services, different types of data can be integrated and different types of maps can be created. This information can be broken down into four categories—victim services, criminal justice, health and social services, and generic.

Examples of victim services data include

- VOCA-funded subgrantee locations and catchment areas.

- Other victim services programs by location and catchment areas.

- Funding of services by multiple funding sources.

- Types of services available by location.

- Locations of claimants for crime victim compensation (awarded and denied).

- Dollar amounts of compensation claims awarded by geographic area.

- Number of victims served by compensation programs.

- Number of victims served by victim services organizations.

Examples of criminal justice data include

- Number of crime incidents.

- Types of crime incidents.

- Locations of police stations, substations, and patrols.

- Computer-aided dispatch calls.

- Firearms purchases.

- Locations of prisons and jails.

- Locations of criminal and juvenile courts.

- Open-air drug markets.

- Gang locations.

- Jurisdictional lines for state police, county sheriffs, tribal police, and municipal police.

- Number of protective or restraining orders.

Examples of health and social services data include

- Locations of public assistance agencies.

- Locations of public housing.

- Locations of hospitals and emergency rooms.

- Locations of mental health programs.

- Locations of youth shelters.

Examples of generic data include

- Census data.

- Neighborhood boundaries.

- State, county, and Indian Country boundaries.

- School locations.

- Business locations.

- Transportation routes.

- Park and recreation areas.

Getting Started

It is easy to talk about what GIS will do, but getting started is another matter. Recognizing this, there are a couple of steps to consider. First, obtain training for staff who will introduce GIS technology to all levels of your agency. Coordinate presentations on what GIS is and what it can do.

Remember, thinking spatially about data is a learned skill. If you spend time teaching the basics of GIS and generate some enthusiasm about the concept, you can avoid a lot of confusion and reluctance down the road. Remember, GIS is a tool that enables an agency to make better use of the data it is already collecting.

Second, perform a needs assessment. A needs assessment is simply a methodological evaluation of an agency's existing needs, resources, and goals. It is a structured approach by which an organization is prompted to ask the right questions when considering implementing a GIS system. Some basic questions to consider are highlighted below.

What Are the Needs and Goals of Our Agency?

To build a GIS system to address the needs of your agency, you must first identify those needs. How will you use GIS? Will you use it to support management decisions, to evaluate existing initiatives and projects, and/or as a predictive modeling tool to identify the location of future subgrants? You can use a GIS system for all of these purposes and more, but knowing what you want to do before you begin will help you define the data needed to support the application.

What Types of Queries Do We Want Supported by the GIS Application?

If you purchase an off-the-shelf GIS software package, the system likely will contain an ad hoc[14] type of querying capability. In other words, any data that you have loaded or integrated into the system can be accessed and queried. However, you may choose to customize the application to address your specific needs. For example, here are two types of query options: One is the ad hoc query used by ArcView 3.1 (exhibit 17) and the other is a screen shot of a customized query[15] built for Connecticut's New Haven Police Department (exhibit 18).

As you can see, a generic query builder is much more flexible but requires more technical expertise and knowledge about the data. A customized query builder requires less training but is more data restrictive. The user only has access to the data fields defined by the

Exhibit 17: Ad Hoc View Used by ArcView 3.1

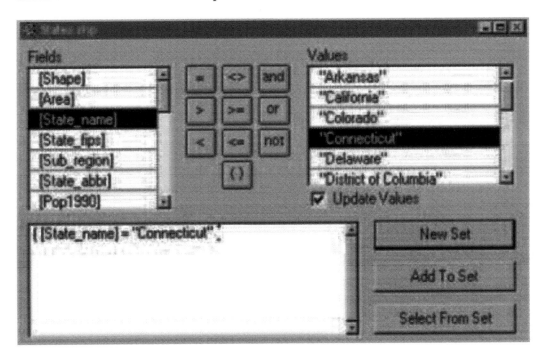

drop-down menu. In the New Haven query menu, users can access several tables but are limited to the particulars of the crime, date, age, time, and day of the week. However, the tables contain much more information than what the menu is displaying (exhibit 18).

What Are Base Maps and Where Can We Get Them?

Base maps are the foundation of a GIS. Typically, they comprise a street centerline and a geographic backdrop such as the census tract, ZIP Code, and/or county and state boundaries. Street centerlines of almost every city, state, or region can be purchased from vendors or downloaded free from the Internet by accessing the U.S. Census Bureau TIGER Files at www.census.gov. TIGER (Topologically Integrated Geographic Encoding and Referencing) is a nationwide, seamless, digital map. Most city information systems departments or planning departments also have centerline files they may be willing to share, especially with other government agencies or nonprofit organizations. These locally generated centerline files tend to be more accurate and detailed because they are created at the local level and are updated more often than the Census Bureau's.

What Additional Data Needs To Be Collected To Support the Application?

In addition to using your own data, you may want to integrate additional data from other sources, such as census figures, law enforcement data, and transportation information. VOCA administrators may choose to collect and share information across state boundaries and between compensation and assistance programs to minimize repetition and duplicate

Exhibit 18: Customized Query for the New Haven Police Department

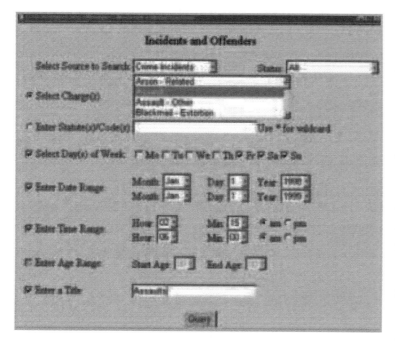

efforts. Some agencies will share information about a case or a person depending on how relevant it is to their agency and privacy concerns. Of course, any information shared should not be identifiable to a specific individual. The only instance in which this should occur would be if more than one agency is working with crime victims and the information sharing is allowed by state law or by informed consent of the victims.[16]

What Are Our Data Formats and How Can We Integrate Disparate Datasets?

Mapping systems can integrate various data formats.[17] However, the most common format is that of a database file, a file extension ending in *.dbf*. Fortunately, most spreadsheet tables can be converted easily to database files to make them ready for integration into a GIS. You can usually convert them by choosing "save as" under the file drop-down menu of your software, choosing a *.dbf* file extension, and following the steps prompted by the application.

Privacy and Confidentiality

NIJ's MAPS, through a contract with the Institute for Law and Justice (ILJ), developed the guide *Privacy in the Information Age: Guidelines for Sharing Crime Maps and Spatial Data* to address privacy and data confidentiality when using GIS. The report is available for downloading from ILJ's Web site at www.ilj.org, and hard copies are available from NIJ. The guidelines discuss options and requirements for addressing privacy, confidentiality, and data sharing and address concerns about the dissemination of geocoded data and the balance between the public's right to know and the victim's right to privacy. The report outlines some of the mechanisms and techniques used to protect privacy and provides Web resources for online mapping efforts.

Although creating a database warehouse for GIS would involve the input of a multitude of data, it would eliminate redundant data collection by agencies. A VOCA database could contain information on crime incidents, victims and offenders, locations of subgrantee recipients, compensation recipients, victim services programs, census data, and jurisdictional and state boundaries. Obviously, data from various organizations will exist in differing formats, but recent technologies make data conversions very easy.

Is Our Data Accurate and Timely?

It is critical that you know your data before using it in GIS. For example, does your community have a Martin Luther King Boulevard? If so, how is it listed? MLK Blvd., Martin Luther King Street, MLK Jr., or another variation? All these options are correct, but their variation may create difficulties when you try to geocode your data. This is a problem many users face when they begin to use their data in a spatial environment. Most agencies have been collecting address-level data for years. Generally, the quality of this data has been left to the discretion and integrity of the person entering the data. The accuracy and standardization of this data will contribute to the overall ease or difficulty with which the data is integrated into your GIS. Another issue to consider is the timeliness of data. Street files may only need to be updated once a year, depending on the construction in the community, but records containing crime incidents, arrests, and claims and subgrant award data may need to be updated more frequently.

What Are Our Hardware and Software Requirements?

Some of the above questions can be answered by staff members who are familiar with the data your agency collects. However, when it comes to hardware and software requirements, it is better to consult with information technology (IT) professionals who can help you define your GIS requirements based on your business needs and budget. IT professionals can help identify the technical needs involved with implementing a GIS. For example, a GIS can be implemented on the Internet, the Intranet, or as a stand-alone application loaded on an agency's personal computer (PC). IT professionals can tell you whether you should add more PCs to your department, install larger transmission lines for faster data transfers, or increase the RAM (random-access memory) and hardware space on your existing PCs. They can also evaluate your assets. Do you have an Intranet that can be used, firewalls in place for confidential data, or other types of security that can be accessed such as password-protected applications? Other issues to be addressed in a needs assessment include training for users, the experience of support personnel, system maintenance, and software licenses.

The GIS package purchased for your program will have greater use if it is compatible with that of other agencies' data. For efficiency's sake, purchase software that can easily export and import GIS files into the appropriate software packages. VOCA administrators and subgrantees within the same state should purchase systems that use the same format for storing data to significantly reduce duplication of effort.

Building a GIS from scratch takes time, effort, and experience, but with today's off-the-shelf desktop mapping applications, developing and customizing a system to address specific organizational goals is relatively routine.

Training Resources Available

Information and Training

Three publicly funded agencies offer free training courses to help law enforcement personnel master crime-mapping technology. VOCA administrators can also take these courses and adapt the information to victim services planning.

The Crime Mapping and Analysis Program (CMAP) at the University of Denver in Colorado offers a 2-week introductory course and courses in more advanced applications. For course schedules and other information, contact Noah Fritz by phone at 1–800–416–8086, by fax at 303–871–2500, or by e-mail at nfritz@du.edu. The CMAP Web site address is www.nlectc.org/cmap.

The Carolinas Institute for Community Policing (CICP) offers courses that emphasize crime mapping technology as an element of community policing. The courses are offered in six cities throughout North and South Carolina in both technical and nontechnical formats. The technical portion is appropriate for crime analysts; the nontechnical portion is appropriate for officers, administrators, and community members. For course schedules and other information, contact Linda Waddell at CICP, Charlotte-Mecklenburg, North Carolina, Police Department, by phone at 704–336–4899, by fax at 704–336–7799, or by e-mail at pdlw@mail.charmeck.nc.us.

Mapping and Analysis for Public Safety (MAPS), in collaboration with the Office of Community Oriented Policing Services, offers training in crime mapping through Regional Community Policing Institutes. The center offers four courses that are appropriate for police officers, crime analysts, community members, and researchers.

Tuition is free and training is held at Regional Community Policing Institutes throughout the country. The courses can be downloaded from the MAPS Web site. To learn about how to become a trainer, how to host training classes, or how to take the training, contact Richard Lumb, CICP Director, Charlotte-Mecklenburg Police Department, by phone at 704–336–2162, by fax at 704–336–7799, or by e-mail at rlumb@cmpd.ci.charlotte.nc.us.

The courses include

Crime Mapping for Community Policing and Problem Solving (4 hours): geared toward officers, community members, and others who are interested in the basics of crime mapping.

Mapping for Managers (4 hours): geared toward administrators and managers who want to know about crime mapping, what to ask for, and what to expect.

What Is Crime Mapping? (8 hours): geared toward analysts, officers, community members, and others who want a more indepth look at crime mapping.

Integrating GIS Into an Organization (8 hours): geared toward analysts, officers, and others who are playing a role in implementing crime mapping in their agency.

Other Resources

Other resources are available to help administrators of crime victim services in their efforts to use crime-mapping technology. The following programs are available to provide onsite technical assistance on GIS to VOCA administrators.

Technical Assistance

The Justice Information Systems Technical Assistance Program provided through SEARCH offers technical assistance to state and local justice agencies in how to acquire, develop, manage, improve, and integrate their automated information systems. SEARCH works with individual justice agencies (such as a police department implementing a new records management system or a court acquiring a new case management system) and with multidisciplinary groups of justice agencies to help them plan for and integrate their information systems at state, local, and regional levels. For more than 20 years, SEARCH programs have provided both onsite and in-house, no-cost technical assistance to justice agencies throughout the country. For more information, go to www.search.org/tech-assistance/default.asp.

Criminal Justice Statistical Analysis Centers

The Justice Research and Statistics Association (JRSA) is a nonprofit organization created in 1974 to promote the use of research in policy decisions and to facilitate the exchange of criminal justice information among states. JRSA's 50 constituent Statistical Analysis Centers are located in almost every state and territory, where they conduct objective analyses to meet planning needs and address statewide policy issues. The association also maintains a clearinghouse of state criminal justice research and programs, conducts multistate research, provides training and technical assistance, and convenes national conferences.

University Statistics and Research Center

An alternative resource for consultation could be a statistics and research center at a nearby college or university. Some examples are undergraduate or graduate schools of public administration, social work, criminal justice science, and public health.

University Statistics and Research Internships

Agencies that are interested in using crime mapping may want to recruit interns from the local university or college to help them in administrative and strategic planning efforts.

Funding GIS Development and Technical Assistance

VOCA

A major OVC responsibility is to administer the Crime Victims Fund, which is derived from fines and penalties paid by federal criminal offenders. Nearly 90 percent of the money collected each year is distributed to states to help fund their victim assistance and compensation programs. These programs help victims and their families.

Through the State Compensation and Assistance Division, OVC administers two formula/block grant programs: Victim Assistance and Victim Compensation. During the past decade, these two programs have improved the accessibility and quality of services to crime victims nationwide.

Approximately 10,000 community-based organizations across the Nation provide services to crime victims. VOCA victim assistance funds, awarded to states each year, support 4,000 such organizations. Priority must be given to victims of sexual assault, domestic violence, and child abuse. In addition, state grantees must give priority to underserved victims of violent crime, such as survivors of homicide victims and victims of assault, robbery, burglary, hate crimes, drunk drivers, fraud, and elder abuse, among others.

All states and territories receive an annual VOCA victim assistance grant. Each state, the District of Columbia, and the territories of the U.S. Virgin Islands and Puerto Rico receive a base amount of $500,000. The territories of American Samoa, Guam, and the Northern Mariana Islands each receive a base amount of $200,000. Additional funds are distributed based on population.

In addition, all 50 states, the District of Columbia, the U.S. Virgin Islands, Puerto Rico, and Guam have established victim compensation programs. Each year, OVC offers eligible programs a grant equal to 40 to 60 percent of the amount the program has awarded to crime victims from state revenue sources in the previous year. Every compensation program reimburses victims for crime-related expenses, such as medical costs, mental health counseling, funeral and burial costs, and lost wages or loss of support when other financial resources such as private insurance or restitution are not available. The program must be operated by a state or territory and offer compensation to victims and survivors of victims of compensable crimes, including crimes involving terrorism, drunk driving, and domestic violence.

Each state VOCA grantee may retain up to 5 percent of each year's grant to administer VOCA victim assistance and compensation grant programs. State administrative dollars may be used to expand, enhance, and/or improve the state's previous level of effort in administrating the VOCA grant programs at the state level and to support activities and costs that affect the delivery and quality of services to crime victims throughout the state. In this context, VOCA administrative funds may be used to support GIS efforts, such as purchasing software, attending relevant training and technical assistance meetings, and paying salaries and benefits for staff and consultants' fees to administer a GIS project.

Byrne Funds

The Bureau of Justice Assistance has one discretionary program, the Byrne Discretionary Grant Program. Under this program, technical assistance and training grants can be awarded to states, local units of government, Indian tribes and tribal organizations, individuals, educational institutions, private nonprofit organizations, and private commercial organizations. Some discretionary awards are competitive, with a limited amount of funds made available to a number of potential recipients. Byrne discretionary funds are awarded directly to criminal justice agencies and private nonprofit organizations to support a comprehensive range of developmental and demonstration projects, technical assistance and training, and public awareness activities and publications.

STOP Violence Against Women Formula Grants

The STOP (Services*Training*Officers*Prosecutors) Violence Against Women Formula Grants Program promotes the development and implementation of effective, victim-centered law enforcement, prosecution, and court strategies to address violent crimes against women. The program is dedicated to the development and enhancement of victim services that involve victims of domestic violence, sexual assault, and stalking.

Technology initiatives are encouraged under the STOP formula program and may include "Developing, installing, or expanding data collection and communication systems, including computerized systems, linking police, prosecution, and the courts or for the purpose of identifying and tracking arrests, protection orders, violations of protection orders, prosecutions, and convictions for violent crimes against women, including the crimes of sexual assault and domestic violence."[18]

Notes

1. A collection of data organized specifically for rapid search and retrieval.

2. A spatial or geographic identifier refers to a location that can be defined geographically (e.g., street addresses, block groups, neighborhoods, police districts, state or county boundaries).

3. A census tract is a boundary created by the U.S. Census Bureau that divides counties into subdivisions that usually range in population from 2,500 to 8,000.

4. A polygon is any shape that is totally enclosed (e.g., circle, square) or any irregular shape that can be defined, such as census tracts, state or county boundaries, and school districts.

5. When a database is linked to the graphics software, integrated disparate datasets are referred to as layers of information because they are displayed in map form.

6. Features are items such as schools, roads, bus stops, churches, or service providers referenced in a query.

7. A street centerline refers to the GIS street file with street name and block ranges attached in a database.

8. Cartography is the art or science of making maps.

9. For more information about crime mapping, visit the MAPS Web site at www.ojp.usdoj.gov/nij/maps.

10. Spatially contextualizing the data refers to layering information in an attempt to reveal new or previously unrecognized relationships that exist between disparate datasets, such as crime and public housing.

11. The Community Policing Beat Book software was developed under a cooperative agreement between NIJ and ESRI. The application, user manual, and relevant documents can be downloaded at www.ojp.usdoj.gov/cmrc/tools/welcome.html.

12. Although the general walking distance to a bus route is approximately ¼ mile, this distance depends on various factors, such as age, neighborhood conditions, and accessibility for people with disabilities.

13. Networking takes into consideration one-way streets, speed limits, and traffic congestion. This technique is used by MapQuest.

14. Ad hoc is a user-defined query that allows you to select specific data from all of the data integrated into the GIS.

15. A customized query is one that is predefined based on user needs; the user does not have access to all data.

16. Data sharing information can be found at www.search.org/integration/pdf/ExchangePoints.pdf.

17. Examples of different data formats that a GIS can integrate include text files generated from word processors such as WordPerfect, Microsoft Word, and WordPad; spreadsheet files generated from software such as Excel, Quattro Pro, and Lotus; and .dbf files such as Access, Paradox, and dBASE V.

18. Violence Against Women Office, *STOP Violence Against Women Formula Grant Program Fiscal Year 2002 Application Guidelines*, U.S. Department of Justice, Violence Against Women Office, 2001.

BIBLIOGRAPHY

Crime Mapping and Data-Driven Management Task Force. 1999. *Mapping Out Crime: Providing 21st Century Tools for Safe Communities.* Washington, DC: U.S. Department of Justice, National Partnership for Reinventing Government.

Green, S.W. 1990. "Approaching Archaeological Space." In *Interpreting Space: GIS and Archaeology,* edited by Kathleen M.S. Allen, Stanton W. Green, and Ezra B.W. Zubrow, 3–8. New York, NY: Taylor & Francis.

Harries, Keith D. 1999. *Mapping Crime: Principle and Practice.* Washington, DC: U.S. Department of Justice, Office of Justice Programs, National Institute of Justice, Crime Mapping Research Center.

Kelling, George L. 1997. *Fixing Broken Windows, Restoring Order and Reducing Crime in Our Communities,* 19. New York, NY: Simon & Schuster.

La Vigne, Nancy, and Julie Wartell. 1998. *Crime Mapping Case Studies: Successes in the Field* (Volume 1). Crime Mapping Research Center, Washington, DC: Police Executive Research Forum.

La Vigne, Nancy, and Julie Wartell. 2000. *Crime Mapping Case Studies: Successes in the Field* (Volume 2). Crime Mapping Research Center, Washington, DC: Police Executive Research Forum.

Mamalian, Cynthia, and Nancy La Vigne. 1999. *The Use of Computerized Crime Mapping by Law Enforcement: Survey Results.* Research Preview. Washington, DC: U.S. Department of Justice, Office of Justice Programs, National Institute of Justice.

Robinson, Arthur H., Joel L. Morrison, Phillip C. Muehrcke, A. Jon Kimerling, and Stephen C. Guptill. 1995. *Elements of Cartography*. Sixth Edition. New York, NY: John Wiley & Sons, Inc.

Weisburd, David, and Tom McEwen. 1997. "Crime Mapping Crime Prevention." In *Crime Prevention Studies* (Volume 8). Monsey, NY: Criminal Justice Press.

ADDITIONAL RESOURCES

Antenucci, John, Kay Brown, Peter Croswell, Michael Kevany, with Hugh Archer. 1991. *Geographic Information Systems: A Guide to the Technology.* New York, NY: Van Nostrand Reinhold.

Block, Carolyn and Lynn Green. 1994. *The Geoarchive Handbook: A Guide for Developing a Geographic Database as an Information Foundation for Community Policing.* Chicago, IL: Illinois Criminal Justice Information Authority.

Block, Carolyn, and Margaret Dabdoub. 1993. *Workshop on Crime Analysis Through Computer Mapping Proceedings: 1993.* Chicago, IL: Illinois Criminal Justice Information Authority.

Block, Carolyn, and Louise Miller. 1983. *Manual for the Pattern Description of Time Series, Part 1: Guide to Pattern Description.* Chicago, IL: Illinois Criminal Justice Information Authority.

Boggs, Sarah L. 1965. "Urban Crime Patterns." *American Sociological Review* 30:899–908.

Brantingham, Paul J., and Patricia L. Brantingham. 1981. *Environmental Criminology.* Prospect Heights, IL: Waveland Press.

Brantingham, Paul J., and Patricia L. Brantingham. 1984. *Patterns in Crime.* New York, NY: Macmillan.

Clarke, Keith C. 1997. *Getting Started With Geographic Information Systems.* Upper Saddle River, NJ: Prentice Hall.

Clarke, Keith C. 1995. *Analytical and Computer Cartography.* Englewood Cliffs, NJ: Prentice Hall.

Dent, Borden D. 1990. *Cartography: Thematic Map Design*. Dubuque, IA: William C. Brown.

Eck, John, and David Weisburd. 1995. *Crime and Place*. Monsey, NY: Willow Tree Press.

Evans, David J., and David T. Herbert. 1989. *The Geography of Crime*. London, England: Rutledge.

Fotheringham, Stewart, and Peter Rogerson. 1995. *Spatial Analysis and GIS*. Bristol, PA: Taylor & Francis.

Haining, Robert. 1990. *Spatial Data Analysis in the Social and Environmental Sciences*. New York, NY: Cambridge University Press.

Harries, Keith D. 1974. *Geography of Crime and Justice*. New York, NY: McGraw-Hill.

MacEachren, Alan 1995. *How Maps Work: Representation, Visualization, and Design*. New York: Guilford Press

Monmonier, Mark. 1991. *How to Lie With Maps*. Chicago, IL: University of Chicago Press.

Monmonier, Mark. 1993. *Mapping It Out*. Chicago, IL: University of Chicago Press.

Onsrud, Harlan J., and Gerard Rushton. 1995. *Sharing Geographic Information*. New Brunswick, NJ: Center for Urban Policy Research.

Rengert, George F., and John Wasilchick. 1985. *Suburban Burglary: A Time and Place for Everything*. Springfield, IL: Charles C. Thomas.

Simpson, Jeff L. 1989. *Applied Community Research Monograph C3: Visual Display of Statistics*. Alexandria, VA: American Chamber of Commerce Researchers Association.

Tufte, Edward R. 1983. *The Visual Display of Quantitative Information*. Cheshire, CT: Graphics Press.

Tufte, Edward R. 1990. *Envisioning Information*. Cheshire, CT: Graphics Press.

Tufte, Edward R. 1997. *Visual Explanations*. Cheshire, CT: Graphics Press.

Weisburd, David, and Tom McEwen. 1997. *Crime Mapping & Crime Prevention*. Monsey, NY: Willow Tree Press.

GLOSSARY

Ad hoc query: A query fashioned from all available data integrated into the GIS.

Cartography: The art or science of making maps.

Census tract: A boundary created by the U.S. Census Bureau that divides counties into populations ranging from 2,500 to 8,000.

Customized query: A predefined query based on user needs, used with systems in which the user does not have access to all data.

Database: A collection of data organized especially for rapid search and retrieval.

Dataset: When a database is linked to the graphics software, integrated disparate datasets are referred to as layers of information because they are displayed in map form.

Polygon: Any shape that is totally enclosed (e.g., circle, square) or any irregular shape that can be defined, such as census tracts, state or county boundaries, and school districts.

Spatial data: Data that are identified with a geographical location, such as x–y coordinates in latitude and longitude, state plane coordinates, street addresses, census tracts, counties, and ZIP Codes.

Spatial or geographic identifier: A location that can be defined geographically (e.g., street addresses, block groups, neighborhoods, police districts, state or county boundaries).

Street centerline: Lines on a map that represent roads; the yellow dashes that separate a two-way street.

FOR FURTHER INFORMATION

Office for Victims of Crime

U.S. Department of Justice

810 Seventh Street NW.

Eighth Floor

Washington, DC 20531

202–307–5983

Fax: 202–514–6383

Web site: www.ojp.usdoj.gov/ovc

Mapping and Analysis for Public Safety

National Institute of Justice

U.S. Department of Justice

810 Seventh Street NW.

Seventh Floor

Washington, DC 20531

202–514–3431

Web site: www.ojp.usdoj.gov/nij/maps

Web Links

Bureau of Justice Statistics

www.ojp.usdoj.gov/bjs

Center for International Science Information Network

www.ciesin.org

CyberInstitute short course on GIS

www.ngdc.noaa.gov/seg/tools/gis

Digital chart of the world
www.maproom.psu.edu/dcw

Digital maps
http://magic.lib.uconn.edu

EROS Data Center, the clearinghouse for U.S. Geological Survey digital data
http://edc.usgs.gov

Federal Bureau of Investigation
www.fbi.gov

Federal Geographic Data Committee
www.fgdc.gov

Federal Justice Statistics Resource Center
fjsrc.urban.org

Geophysical data
www.ngdc.noaa.gov/ngdc.html

GIS datasets put together by ESRI for the production of live maps
www.esri.com/data/mapdata/index.html

GIS dictionary
www.geo.ed.ac.uk/agidict/welcome.html

GIS education and training
http://campus.esri.com

GIS FAQs
www.census.gov/geo/www/faq-index.html

GIS Guide for the Neophyte
http://ice.ucdavis.edu/local/gis/gis_primer.html

GIS links: Free datasets, standards, U.S. Geological Survey sites, U.S. Census Bureau, etc.
www.pipeline.com/~rking/gis.htm

GIS Support Center
www.state.oh.us/das/dcs/gis/

Global Resource Information Database
www.grid.unep.ch

Map FAQs, products and support data
www.mapfacts.com

MARIS spatial data
www.maris.state.ms.us

Massachusetts GIS site and geographic databases
www.magnet.state.ma.us/mgis/massgis.htm

National Archive of Criminal Justice Data
www.icpsr.umich.edu/nacjd

National Center for Victims of Crime
www.ncvc.org

National Organization for Victim Assistance
www.try-nova.org

Natural Resources Research Information Pages
www4.ncsu.edu/~leung/nrrips.html

Pennsylvania State University, access to spatial data of Pennsylvania
www.pasda,psu.edu

South Carolina Department of Natural Resources GIS Data Clearinghouse Home Page
www.dnr.state.sc.us/gisdata/index.html

Thematic maps
www.oseda.missouri.edu

University of California at Berkeley online map collection and links to other data and
map sources
http://library.berkeley.edu/EART

For Further Information

University of Edinburgh, Scotland, GIS reference database and an elevation data catalog
www.geo.ed.ac.uk/home/gishome.html

University of New Mexico Earth Data Analysis Center
http://edac.unm.edu

U.S. Census Bureau
www.census.gov

U.S. Geological Survey digital map data
http://geology.wr.usgs.gov/wgmt/digdata.html

U.S. Geological Survey on transferring data between systems without any loss
http://mcmcweb.er.usgs.gov/sdts/whatsdts.html

Victim Assistance Online
www.vaonline.org

General Web Resources for Training Seminars and Conferences*

www.urisa.org/meetings.htm

http://msdis.missouri.edu

http://magicweb.kgs.ukans.edu/magic/magic_net.html

www.nsgic.org

www.mapinfo.com

www.esri.com/events

www.ojp.usdoj.gov/cmrc/training/welcome.html

www.nlectc.org/nlectcrm/cmaptrain.html

www.nijpcs.org/upcoming.htm

www.usdoj.gov/cops/gpa/tta/default.htm

http://giscenter.isu.edu/training/training.htm

www.alphagroupcenter.com

*As listed in *Crime Mapping News*, spring 2000, volume 2, issue 2.

Using Geographic Information Systems To Map Crime Victim Services

For copies of this monograph and/or additional information, please contact

OVC Resource Center
P.O. Box 6000
Rockville, MD 20849–6000
Telephone: 1–800–627–6872 or 301–519–5500
(TTY 1–877–712–9279)

Or order OVC publications online at http://puborder.ncjrs.org.
E-mail questions to askovc@ojp.usdoj.gov.
Send your feedback on this service to tellncjrs@ncjrs.org.

Refer to publication number NCJ 191877.

For information on training and technical
assistance available from OVC, please contact

OVC Training and Technical Assistance Center
10530 Rosehaven Street, Suite 400
Fairfax, VA 22030
Telephone: 1–866–OVC–TTAC (1–866–682–8822)
(TTY 1–866–682–8880)

Made in the USA
Columbia, SC
17 January 2018